THE LAWS OF MOTION IN
ANCIENT THOUGHT

T0345990

THE LAWS OF MOTION IN ANCIENT THOUGHT

An Inaugural Lecture

BY

FRANCIS MACDONALD CORNFORD
M.A.

LAURENCE PROFESSOR OF ANCIENT
PHILOSOPHY IN THE UNIVERSITY
OF CAMBRIDGE

CAMBRIDGE
AT THE UNIVERSITY PRESS
1931

CAMBRIDGE
UNIVERSITY PRESS

University Printing House, Cambridge CB2 8BS, United Kingdom

Published in the United States of America by Cambridge University Press, New York

Cambridge University Press is part of the University of Cambridge.

It furthers the University's mission by disseminating knowledge in the pursuit of education, learning and research at the highest international levels of excellence.

www.cambridge.org
Information on this title: www.cambridge.org/9781107635371

© Cambridge University Press 1931

This publication is in copyright. Subject to statutory exception and to the provisions of relevant collective licensing agreements, no reproduction of any part may take place without the written permission of Cambridge University Press.

First published 1931
Re-issued 2014

A catalogue record for this publication is available from the British Library

ISBN 978-1-107-63537-1 Paperback

Cambridge University Press has no responsibility for the persistence or accuracy of URLs for external or third-party internet websites referred to in this publication, and does not guarantee that any content on such websites is, or will remain, accurate or appropriate.

THE LAWS OF MOTION IN
ANCIENT THOUGHT

———❽———

IF the munificent bequest of Sir Percival
Maitland Laurence had come to us half a
century ago, the chair of Ancient Philosophy
would have been filled by Henry Jackson. As
praelector of Trinity College until his appoint-
ment to the professorship of Greek, Jackson
threw his abounding vitality into a task which
the University was not in a position to recognise. The nineteenth century saw in him a
figure to be matched, in weight of scholarship
and force of character, with his all but name-
sake of the eighteenth century, Dr Johnson.
Both were masters of the peculiarly English
wit that is near allied, not to madness, but to
common sense; both were great talkers—

Jackson the more genial of the two, countering folly with a north-country bluntness that did not forget the claims of courtesy. He taught the young scholars of many academic generations to clear their minds of loose thinking and never to leave a stone unturned. Like Socrates, he was content to leave his mark upon the minds of his pupils. His influence lives after him; it will continue to be felt by men who may never read a line he wrote. Influence may be healthy or unhealthy. A good teacher has no wish to impose either his personality or his opinions upon his students. He will go his own way, much concerned to set before himself a high standard of integrity, hardly aware that in doing so he is holding up an example to others. He is rather disconcerted by a too docile flock pattering at his heels, and better pleased when one or another strikes out for a gap in the hedge. Jackson's opinions were not easily shaken, but he could relish an attack upon *The Later Theory of Ideas* by assailants whom he had himself furnished with weapons. Three scholars, who were as deeply in his debt as I am in theirs, must be mentioned here: Richard Archer Hind, James Adam, and Robert Hicks. Outside the academic world, there are men still living in many walks of life, who, if they met Jackson only as the unflagging host, perambulating those rooms in Nevile's Court with a syphon in one hand and a cigar-box in the other, count it an honour that they once received a friendly greeting from a great humanist and a great Englishman.

At Cambridge ancient philosophy means, in practice, Greek philosophy. Impassable barriers of language shut off our study from the ancient philosophies of the East. Causes that may seem less cogent have separated it also from the philosophies of modern Europe, which belong to the department of Moral Science. It is unlikely that our two departments will ever be fused into one; but there might be gain on both sides if some link could be forged between them. I have a word to say about the gain that might accrue to us.

The justification for keeping the ancient and

modern departments distinct lies in the different orientation of their respective interests. The students of Moral Science are partly engaged in learning the history of philosophy since Descartes; but it is their privilege to work under men who are themselves philosophers, bent on the advance of living thought. Such men may very well look back upon the speculation of the last four centuries as leading up to the present situation and pointing forward to the next step. The modern department can be criticised only for the suggestion of its syllabus, that philosophy made a clean start from the moment when Descartes retired into his stove (or whatever his *étuve* may have been) to consider whether anything could be more certain than his own existence. One need not read far in the *Discours de la Méthode* to be assured that Descartes took with him into his retreat a mind stored with an inheritance predetermining the train of reflection he there pursued. You cannot draw a line anywhere across the history of thought and ignore what lies on the further side.

Our own department, on the other hand, turns not to the future, but to the past; our study is purely historical. It is open to us to draw a line at the dark ages and dismiss all that lies on the hither side as irrelevant. Our whole task is to reconstruct what went on in the minds of men whose very bones were dust when Descartes was born. It must be hard to understand Kant without reading Plato, whom Kant had read; but in certain ways it is easier to understand Plato without reading Kant, whom Plato had not read. If we have not enough historical sense to save us from reading back into the *Republic* discoveries announced in the *Critiques*, we had better leave Kant unopened.

I have lately been studying a neoplatonic commentary on the First Book of Euclid, hoping to find out how the Greeks conceived the objects and methods of mathematics. I had not read Euclid since those Victorian schooldays when it was still believed that Euclid's *Elements* were the same thing as the elements of geometry. Since then I have spent my life chiefly in the fifth and fourth centuries before the Christian era, improving my Greek and forgetting my mathematics. From that vantage-ground I see Euclid's marvellous codification of geometry lying before me, a triumph still to be achieved in the afterglow of the Alexandrine age. What the elements of geometry are now supposed to be, I have no idea; but I imagine that the modern mathematician, if he ever glanced at Euclid, would look upon his work as a curiosity of antique literature. Now suppose that I and the most accomplished geometer in Cambridge whose learning of Greek culminated in the Little-go were set in competition to interpret the First Book of Euclid. I would undertake to give a better account of its meaning, just because I know nothing of what Euclid could not have known, whereas in my competitor's mind every term and proposition would be charged with misleading associations. That instance shows how ignorance of later developments may be a positive advantage. Nevertheless, the student of ancient philosophy is well advised not to neglect the history of modern thought. It will be of service to him in two ways.

In the first place, even if he could transport himself bodily into the pre-Christian era, he would take his mind with him—a mind set in the mould of twentieth-century European thought. He must do his best, like Descartes, to detach himself from his own historical setting; and it is certain that, like Descartes, he will not wholly succeed. But the more various the systems he studies, the sooner he will learn that his own preconceptions are not self-evident truths, nor his habits of thought dictated by the nature of things. It will be a help, for instance, to know that the Aristotelian logic embedded in all our current language is not the only possible logic. It may then occur to him to wonder whether Aristotle's logic was not, after all, the invention of Aristotle, inapplicable, perhaps, to some pre-Aristotelian philosophies. This loosening and breaking up of the fabric of preconception is the first gain to be counted on.

The second is this. Modern philosophies,

just because they are so different from the ancient, offer us standpoints for a distant view of our subject. Contrast may reveal how strange those older systems are—stranger than they seem at first acquaintance. That is the truth which I propose, in this lecture, to illustrate from a particular example. If we look beneath the surface of philosophic discussion, we find that its course is largely governed by assumptions that are seldom, or never, mentioned. I mean that groundwork of current conceptions shared by all the men of any given culture and never mentioned because it is taken for granted as obvious. The vision of the world present to the Greek imagination had a structure and perspective of its own, guiding their thought along certain avenues, and shutting out the view in other quarters. When we try to recover the outlook so framed and limited, we shall distort the picture if we unconsciously substitute our own perspective for theirs.*

---

* Since this lecture was written I have come upon the following passage in Dr Whitehead's *Science and the Modern World* (1925), p. 71: 'When you are criticising the philo-

The example I shall try to analyse in some detail is the difference between ancient and modern science in their attitude towards the laws of motion and causality. By modern science I mean a scheme of conception which prevailed in the last hundred years and still prevails, at any rate in Victorian minds like my own, when I fall back into natural ways of thinking, not yet readjusted to the recent revolutions in logic and physics. It does not matter, for my purpose, that the philosophy of science crystallised in Mill's *Logic* or in Herbert Spencer seems antiquated to a younger generation, whose philosophy is, perhaps, rather in a fluid, if not a gaseous, state. All I need is a familiar standpoint for the contrast I wish to bring out.

The task of nineteenth-century science was compactly formulated in one of the 'woolly periods of Dugald Stewart' (as Mr Augustine

sophy of an epoch, do not chiefly direct your attention to those intellectual positions which its exponents feel it necessary explicitly to defend. There will be some fundamental assumptions which adherents of all the variant systems within the epoch unconsciously presuppose'.

Birrell calls them), taken by Mill as the motto for his chapters on Induction:

According to the doctrine now stated, the highest, or rather the only proper object of physics, is to ascertain those established conjunctions of successive events which constitute the order of the universe; to record the phenomena which it exhibits to our observations, or which it discloses to our experiments; and to refer these phenomena to their general laws.

That is to say: we are to begin by looking at the course of Nature and recording what we have seen; to go on with experiment, testing any provisional theory suggested by observation; and to end with the statement of general laws that survive the test. These laws, moreover, are described as 'established conjunctions of *successive* events'. We find, as Mill explains, that one phenomenon or event B seems to follow regularly after another phenomenon or event A. What science is to establish, by more careful observation controlled by experiment, is a formula of invariable succession: A is always followed by

B. 'The invariable antecedent is termed the cause; the invariable consequent, the effect.' *A* is the cause of *B*—this is the general law we were to aim at.

It is true, as Mill remarks, that succession in time is not the only relation in which the phenomena of Nature exist: there is also the relation of simultaneity among co-existent phenomena. But Mill dismisses these uniformities of synchronous phenomena with brief notice. Of such uniformities, he says, the most important are the laws of number and the laws of space, the subject of geometry. The invariability of these laws is, indeed, perfect, for they contain no reference to any variety of facts or events succeeding one another in time. But, for the same reason, nothing can be deduced from them except further laws of space and number. So Mill turns away from these uniformities of co-existence to uniformities of succession, with the remark that, of all truths relating to phenomena, those which relate to the order of their succession are the most valuable to us. 'On a knowledge of these', says Mill, 'is founded every reasonable anticipation of future facts, and whatever power we possess of influencing these facts to our advantage.' It is not enough for us that the laws of space and number are rigorous and universal. We must endeavour to find some law of succession having the same attributes and therefore fit to regulate the discovery of all other uniformities of succession. This he finds in the Law of Causation, and so proceeds to the methods of Induction.

One sentence in this summary recalls that, in the first year of Victoria's reign, Macaulay had discerned in Francis Bacon 'the prophet of Big Business',* and, in a paean of Utility and Progress, had declared that the powers of the ancient philosophers were 'systematically misdirected' in that, although they did not neglect natural science, they did not cultivate it for the purpose of increasing the power, and ameliorating the condition, of man. The science whose logic Mill was to formulate had learnt,

* This phrase is Mr Santayana's, 'The Genteel Tradition at bay', *The Adelphi*, Jan. 1931, p. 313.

perhaps unconsciously, the lesson of utility and progress; and its attention was accordingly fixed on those laws of succession, of cause and effect, which alone (as Mill says) enable us to anticipate future facts and to influence them to our advantage. Greek philosophy, as Macaulay saw, was not bent on influencing future facts to our advantage. The pursuit of knowledge, at this significant epoch in human thought, had come to be dissociated from the pursuit of power and wealth. Some instinct led Thales of Miletus to pervert the useful art of land-measurement into the unpractical science of geometry, and Pythagoras to substitute a theory of numbers, called arithmetic, for that other art of calculating sums of money which is so closely linked with the amelioration of man's condition. Worse still, Greek speculation took geometry in particular—that static science—as the pattern and ideal of all knowledge, and so was stricken with barrenness: 'disdaining to be useful, it was content to be stationary'. Seeking wisdom in a realm where nothing moves or changes and no effect ever follows upon any cause, it was blind to the profitable aspect of the laws of succession among phenomena, and dwelt rather on the uniformities of co-existence.

Perhaps, however, it is as idle to praise the disinterestedness of ancient science as to prefer the science of the last century for its subservience to utility and progress. The cause of the contrast may be traced to material conditions. Aristotle connects the pursuit of wisdom, inspired by wonder to seek knowledge for its own sake, with the achievement of leisure. 'It began', he says, 'when you may say that all the necessaries of life and the things that make for comfort and recreation were already secured.' Hence science, like the free man, had breathing-space to exist as an end in itself. The science of the nineteenth century was, in this respect, anything but free. The impulse to extend man's mastery over the resources of Nature coincided with a great crisis in economic history. Between 1800 and 1914 the population of Europe increased from 180 millions to 452 millions, and the white population in the whole world from 185 millions to 559 millions.* 'In order to meet the needs of such a huge population,' wrote Walther Rathenau, 'there remained only one thing for the peoples to do, and that was to acquire completely new customs and laws of life and work, with the object of increasing material production to the utmost....This was only possible in one way: by a ruthless adaptation of means to end, which greatly increased the effectiveness of human labour and at the same time utilised the product of this labour to the fullest extent' —in a word, the mechanisation of the world. Looking back, we can now see that science was unwittingly harnessed to this enormous effort, not so much to 'ameliorate the conditions of life' as to save Europe from starvation. We who have escaped starvation cannot afford to be anything but grateful for the practical outcome of knowledge, even though the concurrent pursuit of power led straight to the calamity of 1914.

* These figures are taken from Sombart's *Hochkapitalismus,* cited by Count Kessler, *Walther Rathenau,* p. 94.

What concerns us at the moment is that this contrast in material conditions explains the emphasis thrown in the nineteenth century on the laws of cause and effect as the key to power over Nature, and on the conquest of space and time by increase in speed of locomotion. The way had been prepared from the Renaissance onwards. The most brilliant discoveries of the sixteenth and seventeenth centuries had been concerned with the laws of motion: we think of Copernicus and Kepler, Galileo and Newton. At the head of the ancient tradition their counterparts, Thales and Pythagoras, are the founders of the static sciences of geometry and arithmetic. They looked, not for laws of motion and change, but for formulae of associated properties in a field lying beyond any lapse of temporal events.

They also founded the two parallel traditions of the ancient science of Nature. Turning to these first essays in cosmology, we observe that nothing is said about the necessary sequence of cause and effect, and that the problem of motion is neglected in a way already noted by Aristotle as scandalous. The word 'necessity' meant to the philosopher logical necessity, not the supposed compulsion of physical causes; to the ordinary Greek it meant inexorable destiny, above the control even of divine power. The word 'law' is missing from the vocabulary of Greek science. 'Law' suggests a rule of behaviour, an enactment governing the relations between persons or things; it is intimately associated with notions of cause and effect, of action and its consequences. The word (if we exclude its suggestion of the command of a lawgiver) is properly used to describe the truth that death normally follows upon a dose of prussic acid; only by a metaphorical extension can it be applied to the truth that the angles at the base of an isosceles triangle are equal. The first of these truths is concerned with the behaviour of prussic acid and its consequences when brought into contact with animal tissues. The second is not established by watching the conduct of isosceles triangles and contriving experiments to catch them in the act. It tells us only that a certain shape is logically linked with a certain property.

On the other hand, more recent writers on the scope of natural science have denied that it is the sole, or even the main, purpose of science to establish laws of the sequence of cause and effect. Mr Norman Campbell,* for instance, notes that laws in that metaphorical sense we have just noticed—timeless laws of associated properties—bulk largely in the actual content of physical science. The properties of steel, he remarks, 'are not events which follow each other. It is not necessary, in order to prove that a substance is steel, always to observe that it is attracted by a magnet before it is observed that it will rust in damp air; there is no time-relation of any kind between the two properties. The properties of a single substance, the invariable association of which is asserted by the "law" of that substance, are something quite independent of the times at which they are observed. They differ completely in this matter from events which are

* N. R. Campbell, *What is Science?* pp. 52, 56.

related to each other as cause and effect'. Mr Campbell observes further that laws of this type, asserting that there is such a thing as steel, considered as a group or system of constantly associated properties, are, in an elementary and imperfect form, 'the earliest laws of science, and retain their peculiar significance through much of its subsequent development'. They form the content of the classificatory sciences, such as the older zoology, botany, mineralogy, which arranged animals, plants, and minerals in groups according to their resemblances or differences, but did not state about them any laws of the other kind, formulating those conjunctions of *successive events* which Dugald Stewart declared to be the only proper object of physical inquiry.

In reasserting the claims of these timeless formulae of associated properties, Mr Campbell reverts to the standpoint of ancient science. The recognition that 'there is such a thing as iron' leads on to the question: What is iron? The answer is not a law of cause and effect, but a definition. A complete definition would

23

enumerate all the invariable properties which make up the 'being' or essence or nature of iron. Inquiry will aim at isolating and distinguishing this thing from things that superficially resemble it and circumscribing its essential nature.

It is at once clear how closely a science of Nature so conceived approaches to geometry. In Euclid the various figures—triangle, circle, and the rest—are first defined, and then their invariable properties are unfolded by deductive reasoning. If these properties can ever be exhausted, we shall know all there is to know about the nature of the triangle or the circle. It was inevitable that a science of Nature growing up under the shadow of geometry should fall into a like attitude and fix upon the questions, what a thing is in itself and what internal properties it has, to the neglect of the question how it behaves towards other things.

To this account we must add the notion of substance. I have just spoken—we constantly speak—of a thing and its properties, as if we were not content to have enumerated all those characters of which our senses can make us aware, but were constrained, by some blind impulse of faith, to conceive them as 'properties', rooted in an unknowable something which underlies and possesses them. All ancient, and much modern, philosophy has had this notion of the underlying substance among its premisses, whether tacit or avowed; and in despite of all efforts to expel it from philosophy, it remains unshaken in the popular mind. When Aristotle laid bare the anatomy of thought in his *Organon,* this premiss came to light in its logical form: 'Every proposition has a subject and a predicate'; but of course the notion of substance had existed for untold centuries before the terms 'subject' and 'predicate' were invented. Its historical source is to be looked for partly in a projection from our own nature, the ineradicable belief in an essential self, a 'me', which underlies and owns not only my body but my mind, and persists through all changes and processes of experience. When we extend this habit of thought to objects in the outer world, we have the picture of a *thing* or *substance*, as an enduring essence or core of being, with a fringe of properties or attributes, more or less intimately inherent in it and depending on its existence.

What place is there in this picture for the relations between things and the actions constituting their behaviour to one another? These entities cannot be conceived as substances, and they were not allowed an independent status. They were not to subsist *between* two substances without inhering in either: a relation was like a drawbridge, which must be hinged to the pier on one bank and thence let down to make contact with the pier on the other. So relations were assumed to have the status of attributes securely anchored in the independently existing substance.

In particular, those relations of a substance which take the form of its action on other substances were considered under the aspect of powers or capacities of action residing within the substance. The substance carried about with it this battery of powers, like a warship bristling with guns, ready to discharge a projectile when a suitable target is sighted. The complete inventory of a warship would include an account of its guns and ammunition, but not of the laws governing the trajectory of a shell after it has left the muzzle. So, if we are inquiring what a substance is, we shall include an account of its powers or virtues or active properties, but not of relations or laws of cause and effect lying between that substance and other things.

The *Analytics* admirably illustrate the consequence of this attitude in the treatment of those causal laws which have been taken as typical of modern science. The classical example is the eclipse of the moon. Where modern science would ask for a law of cause and effect, Aristotle is at pains to reduce this question to terms of a subject and its attributes. He says in so many words: 'If we ask "Does the moon suffer eclipse?" the question concerns a part of the thing's being; what we are asking is whether a thing has or has not this or that attribute'.* The moon is the subject,

* *Posterior Analytics*, II, 90a.

eclipse is its property; just as the subject 'triangle' may have the property 'equality'. In both examples, he says, it is clear that the nature of the thing and the reason of the fact are identical. The question 'What is eclipse?' and its answer 'The privation of the moon's light by interposition of the earth' are identical with the question 'What is the reason of eclipse?' (or 'Why does the moon suffer eclipse?') and the reply 'Because of the failure of light through the earth's shutting it out'. He concludes that 'to know a thing's nature is to know the reason why it is', and this is equally true, whether we are accounting for the substantive existence of the moon or for the fact that it has an attribute, such as eclipse. In either case our inquiry aims, not at a law of cause and effect, but at a definition.

Aristotle's logic is of special value as bringing to light some of the tacit assumptions of all Greek scientific thought. His handling of the cause of eclipses, perverse as it seems to us, is not a perversity peculiar to Aristotle's mind;

it is in line with all earlier speculation. If we frame a single question which all that speculation was to answer, the question is: 'What is the nature of things—the *rerum natura*, the φύσις τῶν ὄντων?' The schools can be grouped in two main traditions, one of which found the nature of things in their matter, the other in their form. Form and matter are the two pre-eminent 'causes' in Aristotle's sense; but neither is a cause in our sense of the word. They are internal constituents into which the total thing can be analysed. Attention is focussed upon them, and the whole field of relations and interactions between things is comparatively neglected. The *Categories* does not speak of 'relations' at all, but only of 'relative terms' or 'predicates'; and they are illustrated by nouns and adjectives, not by verbs.

But this field cannot, of course, be entirely ignored. A science of Nature must have something to say about the laws of motion and change. What principles do we, in fact, find in possession of this neglected field? The answer is not far to seek: the field is occupied by

29

popular maxims, accepted by philosophy from common sense without scrutiny.

It has often been remarked that the battle is half won when science has got so far as, first, to discover that there is a problem to be solved, and then to formulate that problem correctly. So long as we ask, 'Why does the sun go round the earth in a circle?' we may be content to reply, 'Because the sun is divine, and the circle is the most perfect figure'. The public will applaud our doctrine as obviously right and tending to edification. But when we come to ask, 'Why does the earth go round the sun in an ellipse?' the question and the answer alike may be so revolting to common sense that some of the men of science implicated may be lucky if they are not burnt alive. Now Anaxagoras, it is true, had to leave Athens because he said that the sun was not a god but a mass of incandescent rock; but where the behaviour of divine beings was not concerned, there was nothing outrageous in his theory of motion (if he may be said to have had one), for the principle he invoked was taken straight from popular belief. It was one of a set of maxims expressed or implied in every ancient system that had anything to say about motion. In our histories of philosophy these maxims are mentioned at points when the ancients happen to mention them; but they are passed over without inquiry into their origin and without appreciation of the far-reaching consequences of assuming them as obvious.

Let us consider these maxims more closely. Aristotle distinguishes three species of change: movement from place to place (locomotion); change of quantity (growth and diminution); and change of quality (alteration). Each of these three fields we shall find occupied by a maxim accounting for the changes that occur in it in terms of the *likeness* or *unlikeness* in the nature of the things undergoing change. Thus movement in space is explained by asserting that *Like attracts like*; growth, by asserting that *Like nourishes like*; change of quality, by asserting that *Like affects like*. Nearly every ancient philosopher invokes some principle of this type. The only difference of opinion is on the question whether it is not rather unlike things that attract, or nourish, or affect one another. No one stops to ask if these maxims are well founded or capable of bearing the structure of theory based upon them. Let me justify this statement by a brief review of the evidence.

To begin with locomotion and its maxim, 'Like attracts like'. Both Plato and Aristotle, in their analysis of friendship, start from this topic: 'Does friendship naturally arise between persons who are like one another or unlike?' and both appeal, on the one hand, to proverbial sayings and, on the other, to the application of such maxims to explain motion in systems of cosmology. In Plato's *Lysis* Socrates says:

The poets are like fathers to guide us in the path of wisdom. Naturally what they have to tell us about those between whom friendship exists is impressive. They say it is heaven itself that makes them friends, drawing one to another. They put it, if I remember, in this way: 'Heaven draws ever like to like' and makes them acquainted. . . . You must also have met with treatises by the wisest of men asserting the same thing—that there must always be an attraction between like and like. I mean the men who discourse or write about the nature of things and the universe. (214 A.)

Aristotle echoes the *Lysis*:

Some define friendship as a kind of likeness and say that like persons are friends; hence the sayings: 'Like to like', 'Birds of a feather', and so on.... And in this matter they look for reasons that lie deeper in the nature of things....Empedocles, among others, asserts that like is drawn to like.
(*Nicomachean Ethics*, VIII, 1.)

In Empedocles' system all the phenomena of motion are, in fact, brought under one or another axiom of the type we are considering. The attraction of like to like holds between the scattered parts of any one element:

All of these—sun, earth, sky and sea—are at one with their parts dispersed in mortal things. And so all things that are more fitted for mixture are like to one another and united in love by Aphrodite. (*Frag.* 22.)

The whole rhythm of Empedocles' cosmic machinery is referred to two other principles of the same sort: the mutual attraction between unlikes or contraries, which is Love, and their mutual repulsion, which is Hate or Strife. This is not mere poetical metaphor or allegory; it is the whole content of his doctrine of motion. The principle that like is drawn to like figures equally in the severely prosaic systems of Anaxagoras and the Atomists. Anaxagoras dispenses with the Love and Hate of Empedocles, but he explains the emergence of distinct natural substances out of the indiscriminate mixture by the fact that 'things of the same kind move towards one another'. He shares with the Atomists the notion of a world-forming vortex, and, like the Atomists, was no doubt influenced by the simple observation that bodies floating in water tend to congregate at the centre of an eddy.

Democritus, we are told, set up this principle of like to like as universal both in living and inanimate things.

'All animals alike', he says, 'herd together with their own kind—doves with doves and cranes with cranes. And so is it also with inanimate things, as you may see in the case of grains shaken in a sieve, or the pebbles on the sea-shore. The whirling motion of the sieve arranges the grains in distinct groups—lentils with lentils, barley with barley, wheat with wheat; and the motion of the waves rolls all the long-shaped pebbles into one place, all the round ones into another, showing that the likeness of things tends to draw them together'. (*Frag.* 164.)

So too his predecessor Leucippus had said that the atoms circling in the cosmic eddy 'were separated apart, like to like'.

There are two points of general interest here. One is the part played by observation and experiment in ancient science. Some writers, anxious to credit the Greeks with the anticipation of modern methods, catch at every appeal they make to observation and the few recorded instances of so-called experiment. But an unbiassed view of the evidence shows that observations, like that of the sifted grain, are not the basis on which the theory is formed, but casual illustrations called in to support a principle already assumed as obvious. Democritus never thinks of analysing the phenomenon of the sifted grain into mechanical laws of motion, or of probing into the question why the action of water sifts out the round pebbles. A little more curiosity might have taken him so far as to visit a beach and see whether, after all, the round pebbles are actually separated from the long ones. He might then have discovered that pebbles are sorted rather by size than shape; and that might have suggested that their weight had something to do with their distribution. But perhaps the coast off Abdera was too rocky; so Democritus sat at home seeing quite clearly that pebbles or atoms of like shape must come together.

In the same way the experimental proofs devised by the ancients are contrived to illustrate a foregone conclusion. The author of the medical treatise *On the constitution of children**accounts for the development of all the various parts of the body from the seed by our principle that like things come together— dense to dense, rare to rare, and so on: 'each thing moves into its proper place according to its own affinity'. To convince the reader that

* Hippocrates, περὶ φύσιος παιδίου, 17 (Littré, vii, 496).

this is so, he recommends him to attach a pipe to a bladder containing earth and sand and lead filings. Then pour in water, and blow through the pipe. At first all the substances will be mixed up in the water; later the lead will come to the lead, the sand to the sand. Allow them to dry, and open your bladder. You will find that like has come to like.

This is not an experiment in the modern sense. There is no purpose of interrogating Nature and abiding by the unforeseen answer she will deliver. It is no more than the construction of a mechanical model. The author never asks if the processes of organic growth can be purely mechanical, or why like things should come together, or what sort of likeness is required. Once more, nothing is said about differences of weight. The so-called experiment does not put a question; it illustrates a principle taken as already known.

Both these instances suggest another point of far-reaching significance. The acceptance of the popular notion that like moves to like barred the path to a science of mechanics by diverting attention from the property of weight, which never comes by its own. The difference between light and heavy things is of such obvious practical importance when we try to move them about that one might expect these properties to bulk large in early cosmology. But in fact they do not; and one reason seems to be that the phenomena of motion, thanks to our maxim, were too closely associated with qualitative resemblances of hotness and coldness, wetness and dryness and the rest, or (as in the Atomists) with likenesses of shape. Hence we find that heaviness and lightness are treated as (so to say) incidental epithets describing the behaviour of substances which is essentially due to the tendency of like things to get together. So Plato rests content with Empedocles' principle that the scattered parts of each element are always seeking to rejoin the main mass.

When we weigh earthy substances, we are lifting them into an unlike region (the air) forcibly against their natural tendency, and they cling to their own kind; but the lesser bulk is more readily constrained than the greater, and moves more quickly into the unlike region. Hence we have come to call such a bulk 'light' and the region to which we constrain it 'up', and to call the opposites 'heavy' and 'down'.... So these determinations must be variable and relative.... The passage of each body towards the kindred aggregate gives the name 'heavy' to the moving body, and 'down' to the direction of the movement.

(*Timaeus*, 63 c.)

Aristotle again will not allow heaviness and lightness to be primary properties or powers of matter; they are consequent upon the tendency of the simple bodies to make for their proper region. So long as the fall of the apple to the ground was satisfactorily explained by the impulse of its earthy nature to seek reunion with the kindred mass of earth, the laws of motion were likely to remain a secret.

The influence of these maxims extended to the two other types of change distinguished by Aristotle. Change of size is chiefly important in connection with processes of nutrition and growth in organic bodies. Here Empedocles, Anaxagoras, and Plato all invoke the cosmic principle of like to like. I need only quote the *Timaeus*:

All the tissues, as they are irrigated with the blood, repair what they have lost by evacuation. The character of this depletion and repair is the same as that of the movement in the universe, whereby all things move towards their own kind. (81 A.)

The third type of change—alteration of quality—is of wider significance. Here the maxim takes the form, 'Like acts on (affects) like', in the sense of modifying its qualities. Democritus held that 'agent and patient must be the same or alike; for if different things act on one another, it is only accidentally by virtue of some identical property'.* Most other philosophers took the opposite view that, if things are to affect one another, they must be unlike. They instanced the familiar fact that when my hands are cold the heat of the fire

* Aristotle, *De gen. et corr.* 323 *b*, 10, says that Democritus alone maintained that only like could act on like; but elsewhere he recognises this principle in Empedocles' doctrine of perception (cf. Prof. Joachim *ad loc.*). Theophrastus, *de sensibus*, 39, attributes it also to Diogenes of Apollonia.

will warm them; their state is not modified by contact with things of the same temperature.

On the other hand, in one important application the principle 'Like affects like' had a wider vogue. It figures in early theories of knowledge. As Sextus (*adv. Math.* VII, 116) says, 'the physical philosophers have a doctrine of high antiquity that like things are capable of knowing one another'. It must be remembered that sensation and sense-perception were at first taken as typical of all forms of knowledge, and indeed not distinguished from judgement or thinking. Aristotle remarks:

Soul, we are told, consists of the elements, in order that it may perceive and know each several thing. It is assumed that like is known by like, and so the soul is identical with the things it knows....Perceiving is supposed to be the same as being affected in some way or moved, and so are thinking and knowing. (*de anima*, 409*b*, 24.)

So Empedocles said: 'By earth (in our sense-organs) we see earth (outside us), by water, water', and so on.

Diogenes of Apollonia held that the soul

was air, the primary element of all things, and hence could know all things. And the same principle is implied in the construction of the soul in the *Timaeus* (37).

Where perception is explained by effluences passing from object to sense-organ, this theory of cognition is reinforced by the axiom of locomotion, that like moves to like. But Theophrastus adds another ground still more naive and popular: 'It is natural to all living creatures to become acquainted with (recognise) creatures of their own kind' (*de sensibus*, 1). So, through the associations of 'acquaintance', 'like knows like' is linked with the familiarity, affinity, friendship between things of the same kind from which we started.

I have not time to review, in the same detail, the opposed series of maxims asserting the same relations to hold, not between like things, but between unlikes or contraries. I will only quote once more Plato's *Lysis* on this side of the question:

I have heard someone say that between like things there is (not friendship but) the greatest possible enmity. He cited Hesiod: 'Potter bears a grudge against potter, minstrel against minstrel, beggar against beggar', and so, he said, it must always be: the greater the likeness between things, the more they must be filled with jealousy, rivalry, and hostility towards one another; the greater the unlikeness the stronger the attraction....Everything desires, not its like but its contrary: the dry desires moisture, the cold warmth, the bitter sweetness, the sharp dullness, the empty to be filled, the full to be emptied, and so on. For one contrary finds its nourishment in the other; the like can get no benefit from the like. (215 c.)

The quotation reveals that the basic notion in this series of axioms is different. We are not now to think of the solidarity binding together a herd of animals or any group of similar things. The doctrine of contraries appeals to the experience of desire, the longing of the incomplete for the complement it lacks. Aristotle in his parallel passage (*E.N.* VIII, 1) cites Euripides: 'The parched Earth desires the rain, and desire moves the Heaven, when filled with rain, to fall upon the Earth', and the marriage of Earth and Heaven gives birth to all life

43

(*Frag.* 898). This is the operation of Aphrodite and Eros, at work between the typical contraries, male and female, without which, as Heracleitus said, no life could exist. All this side of the matter we must leave, noting only that where Aristotle turns to consider the cause of motion he observes:

One might suspect that the first to look for such a cause was Hesiod or whoever else ranked Eros or desire as a principle in existing things, like Parmenides:

> 'First of all the gods she devised Eros'.

> (*Met.* 984*b*, 23.)

The explanation of cosmic motion by desire comes out most clearly in the system of Empedocles, whose principle of Love, openly called Aphrodite, embodies in material form the mutual attraction of contraries.

It would be interesting to trace these maxims back still farther and observe their working as the unacknowledged principles of magic. It is at once obvious that the affinity of like things and their influence on one another lies at the root of sympathetic magic. The ancient

Hindoos used yellow parrots to cure jaundice; the yellowness of the bird would attract the yellowness out of the patient. The Greeks believed that the same disease could be cured by catching the yellow eye of the stone curlew. Plutarch says, 'Such is the bird's nature and temperament that it draws out and receives the malady, which issues, like a stream, through the eyesight'.* When the latest philosophers came to take account of magic, they recognised that it was founded on the mysterious affinities and oppositions of Nature. Plotinus asks:

How are magical practices to be explained? By sympathy, by the existence of a concordance of like things and a contrariety of unlike things, and by a diversity of many operative powers in the one living universe. Without any external contrivance, there is much drawing and spell-binding. The true magic is the Love and Strife in the uni-

* J. G. Frazer, *Lectures on the Early History of the Kingship* (1905), p. 47. Our study suggests that the psychological basis of sympathetic magic is to be sought rather in the field of instinctive emotions—the herd instinct, sexual attraction and repulsion—than in the intellectual association (or failure in dissociation) of ideas.

verse (*Philia* and *Neikos*—Empedocles' terms); in magical practices men turn this to their own uses.

(*Ennead*, IV, 4, 40.)

All mimetic rites, such as rain-making, might be brought under the formula 'Like influences like', though not till conscious speculation has begun can we expect the formula to be reduced to abstract and general terms. When we do find it so stated in the earlier philosophies, we must not mistake it for a principle derived by any rational process from the observation of Nature. That is one point that I have wished to bring out. The philosophers themselves appeal to current proverbs and the gnomic wisdom of the poets. And rightly; for in historic fact, the moral and human meaning of the maxims is older than their application to physics. They expressed psychological truths long before they usurped the place that was one day to be filled by scientific laws of motion and change.

We have seen how wide was the field in which a facile acceptance of these traditional axioms disguised the nature of the problems to be formulated and solved. They covered the consideration of the causes and laws of motion in space and of qualitative change, physiological processes of growth and nutrition, a substantial part of medical theory, and even the doctrine of the nature of knowledge. That their reign was undisturbed throughout the ancient period was due, as I said at the outset, to the habit of inquiring after the nature of things and their inherent properties rather than their behaviour and relations. In philosophy, after all, as distinct from natural science, there may be something to be said for this attitude. The knowledge which is wisdom is conceived by Plato as a marriage of the human soul with truth and reality; and it is hard to think of the soul as married to the laws of thermodynamics or a chain of equations.

www.ingramcontent.com/pod-product-compliance
Ingram Content Group UK Ltd.
Pitfield, Milton Keynes, MK11 3LW, UK
UKHW020448010325
455719UK00015B/479